'A   ok with strategies that support early
ye   mote a positive approach to behaviour.
A   time-poor earlier years practitioners)
ai   can dip back in and out of as you
n

ennie Johnson MBE, Chief Executive,
Kids Allowed Limited

Positive Behaviour Management in Early Years Settings

of related interest

How to Be a Great Leader in Early Years
Jennie Johnson
ISBN 978 1 84905 674 8
eISBN 978 1 78450 180 8

Learning Through Child Observation
Third Edition
Mary Fawcett and Debbie Watson
ISBN 978 1 84905 647 2
eISBN 978 1 78450 141 9

Health and Safety in Early Years and Childcare
Contextualising health and safety legislation
within the Early Years Foundation Stage
Bernadina Laverty and Catherine Reay
ISBN 978 1 90939 100 0
eISBN 978 1 90939 117 8

**Observing Children with Attachment
Difficulties in Preschool Settings**
A Tool for Identifying and Supporting Emotional and Social Difficulties
Kim S. Golding, Jane Fain, Ann Frost, Sian Templeton and Eleanor Durrant
ISBN 978 1 84905 337 2
eISBN 978 0 85700 676 9

Listening to Young Children
The Mosaic approach
Alison Clark and Peter Moss
ISBN 978 1 90796 926 3
eISBN 978 1 90796 942 3

Parents, Early Years and Learning
Parents as partners in the Early Years Foundation
Stage – Principles into practice
Helen Wheeler and Joyce Connor
ISBN 978 1 90581 843 3
eISBN 978 1 90581 886 0

Positive Behaviour Management in
Early Years Settings

AN ESSENTIAL GUIDE
by Liz Williams

Jessica Kingsley *Publishers*
London and Philadelphia

First published in 2017
by Jessica Kingsley Publishers
73 Collier Street
London N1 9BE, UK
and
400 Market Street, Suite 400
Philadelphia, PA 19106, USA

www.jkp.com

Library of Congress Cataloging in Publication Data
Names: Williams, Liz (Education consultant), author.
Title: Positive behaviour management in early years settings : an
essential guide / Liz Williams.
Other titles: Positive behavior management in early years settings
Description: London ; Philadelphia : Jessica Kingsley Publishers, 2016.
Identifiers: LCCN 2016025144 | ISBN 9781785920264 (alk. paper)
Subjects: LCSH: Behavior modification. | Classroom management. |
Early
childhood education.
Classification: LCC LB1060.2 .W55 2016 | DDC 371.102/4--dc 3 LC
record available at https://lccn.loc.gov/2016025144

British Library Cataloguing in Publication Data
A CIP catalogue record for this book is available from the British Library

ISBN 978 1 78592 026 4
eISBN 978 1 78450 273 7

Printed and bound in Great Britain

To Keith, Emma and Laura

Acknowledgements

I would like to acknowledge the impact that the work
and principles of Marion Bennathan OBE have had on
my own career and beliefs.

Contents

Introduction

Developing children's social, emotional and behavioural skills can sometimes be a tricky business. The term 'behaviour' itself can be emotive since we all have our own understanding of what the word means and we all have behaviours that we find more or less acceptable within a given context. However, by considering a number of areas in more depth, change can be brought about more easily.

Having worked with both early years providers and schools over many years it became apparent to me that I was being asked the same questions over and over again with regard to behaviour management and that most settings in effect needed similar advice. This is not to say in any way that each provider is the same and that children's situations and circumstances are not unique, rather that the starting points for teaching the skills young children may need seem to be broadly similar. The systems in the end will most probably turn out to be different, as all behaviour happens in a context and is dependent on many factors, including relationships.

This book is designed to be a quick guide, maybe for beginners and those with less experience, maybe for those of us who have been working in the field for years and who would just like to have a quick refresher. All of us are lifelong learners, so no matter what our experience and background, we can always hone our skills and understanding.

Everything in this book is offered for consideration, to be mulled over and to be tested out. In this field there are no hard and fast answers, but there are systems, structures, techniques and approaches that can be of use to staff, parents and children alike. Some of these suggestions and approaches may seem overly simplistic, but they are grounded in research – in evidence of what has been seen to work – and pull together my findings over at least 20 years.

The short chapter headings give an indication of the scope of the book. The book has been kept deliberately short so that it can be read quickly in its entirety, and that is really the way in which I would prefer you to view it; however, the headings are there so that you can have an even quicker look at any particular section if you so wish.

The material in each section should set the reader off in the right direction, in terms of mindset and actions, and is intended as a starting point. The book is written in straightforward language in order to make it accessible and user friendly.

The book was written with nursery staff in mind, whether that be those in independent settings or school nursery classes. It was also written for those new to the filed or who work within early years, as an overview and a starting point. I also feel that it may be of use to parents and to experienced and recently qualified teachers working in the early years sector. None of us have the 'answers' but it's the focus on developing expertise to support young children and develop their skills that counts.

I would welcome any feedback, and thank you for taking a look.

1

Definitions of Behaviour

The first question is – what do we mean by behaviour? Behaviour can be defined as the way in which we act or conduct ourselves, especially towards others: the way in which a person behaves in response to a particular situation, the way we go about things. But it's actually a bit more complex than that.

When behaviour is mentioned in the context of small children, in nurseries or schools, all too often it is because children are not behaving in a way that adults want or like. In other words, the behaviour is negative. There is a perception that this behaviour needs to be 'managed' – hence the title of this book. Turn this into a positive; look at behaviour as a set of skills to be learned and applied in a variety of different situations. This is really the key – look for the positives.

When we focus on the problems and consider the negatives it doesn't really move us on. It is easier to see children's behaviour as simply what they do, how they act and – for practitioners in settings – what we observe. Children's behaviour isn't actually something we should 'manage', it's a set of skills and competencies that we

Children's behaviour is a set of skills and competencies we should strive to help develop.

should strive to help develop. This includes both 'acting out' behaviour and quiet, withdrawn behaviour.

Children begin to learn skills from the minute they are born. In a group of 25 children there are 25 different skill sets, thought patterns, emotions and background influences. All these things have been learned in different ways and at different times, and there are many things still to be developed.

Children who find it difficult to conform in settings and schools for whatever reason have always been around; but over the years the education system has changed, and in many ways become increasingly formal, with less play, less exploration and less time to develop fundamental skills. Historically, children who found it hard to fit in were given different labels; society used to call children who didn't quite fit in with the system maladjusted or, even further back, moral imbeciles – and there have been various theories as to how to support them over time. Now there is a far greater understanding of the different skills small children need to learn and that in fact one size does not fit all. Therefore there may be a need to adjust our systems in order to include everybody, coupled with a need to give experiences that are required. There is also a far greater acceptance of the fact that different children learn in different ways.

When each of us thinks of 'behaviour' we all have a different picture in our heads. Behaviour is subjective – and happens in a situation – with various factors influencing it. My definition of 'good' behaviour may not be yours; it's based on what I find acceptable depending on the situation. Likewise 'inappropriate behaviour'; you may find something inappropriate but I may think that this is fine given the circumstances. The behaviours that I find acceptable in various contexts come from my own experience – the way I was brought up, my core beliefs and the experiences I have had. It is the same for every individual working with children: while we are likely to have elements in common, our reasons for believing this are likely to be slightly different.

The belief that positive behaviour is a set of skills that can be taught/encouraged/supported is central, and our professional practice needs to be fair and not unduly influenced by our own personal values and feelings – as far as this is possible.

When provision actively makes teaching the skills needed for positive behaviour a priority there are fewer 'difficulties' to deal with. This may seem obvious, but it is sometimes an area that does not receive focus until things start to go wrong. A proactive positive approach works best.

2

Why We and Children
Behave as We Do

The only behaviour you can change is your own. You can teach skills, create situations, give advice to prompt others, but in the end the only behaviour you can change yourself is the behaviour that belongs to you. Changing your behaviour has an impact on how others behave around you. Try it – do something differently and see what happens. Sometimes it can be as simple as sitting in a different chair in a meeting or when watching television with your family.

The behaviour of any person – child or adult – depends on a number of factors. It is important to understand that behaviour is situational – it always happens within a context. For adults this may be the context of home, work, social events and so on, and people's behaviour is often subtly different accordingly. Every member of staff in a school or nursery brings their whole self to work each day; they bring their worries, anxieties, enthusiasm and happiness to different degrees at different times.

The quality of relationships is crucial.

Think and reflect

What did you bring with you this morning?

Did you sleep well?

Have you had breakfast?

Are you anxious to get home because there is something on your mind?

Children bring the same sorts of things with them too when they arrive for their session in nursery – and we do not always know what these are.

Behaviour also depends on academic, social and emotional capacity and age and stage of development. Chronological age does not always correlate with emotional and social age and is dependent on context. This is really important to consider. It is perfectly possible, as an adult, to have a toddler tantrum if the situation arises! Just because a child is five years old it doesn't mean that emotionally, in some situations, they won't behave as though they are two years old. Behaviour is not necessarily consistent within the same situations – a person faced with a situation on a 'good' day may manage it well; on a 'bad' day the outcome will be different because of their differing emotional states as the same situation arises.

Our social, emotional and behavioural capacities may well develop at a different rate to our intellectual capacities.

17

As adults we generally understand how to behave and react in different situations – what is appropriate, what isn't, what can be followed up later – and we have learned a degree of self-control and are able to behave 'appropriately'. A small child's world is so much more immediate. They have a tendency to just do it – to just react – as their self-regulatory skills are still beginning to develop.

If we are preoccupied or worried this impacts on our behaviour; likewise if we are tired, hungry or thirsty. It's the same for children. Some mornings a piece of toast can make all the difference.

Different children will see the world differently depending on their previous life experiences. Children with special educational needs – which may or may not have been identified when they are in early years settings – may see the world in yet another different way. For example, children with an Autistic Spectrum Disorder may find it very difficult to build relationships and may become very distressed if routines are not followed to the letter.

The quality of the experiences children have had and the quality of the relationships they go on to build are crucial. They need consistency; firm but flexible boundaries; opportunities to interact, learn and explore at developmentally appropriate levels; the freedom to make mistakes; love; nurturing; and opportunities to develop a sense of self. These are things that adults who care for children can impact upon.

All behaviour is communication. Sometimes as adults we may not immediately understand why the child is behaving as they are. Sometimes we may never understand. Even if we don't understand we can do our best to create the environment and relationships in order for the child to communicate in what may be a more appropriate way. What is the child trying to tell you? It is important that we try to enable children to develop their own sense of right and wrong rather than just to comply with instructions from adults as to how they should behave. The child's behaviour is a way of giving us a message.

Some of the elements which are thought to influence behaviour are difficult or impossible for a setting or school to change. For example, it is impossible to change birth order and physical differences; it is hard to change disposition. However, we can impact on skills, including social coping skills, the quality of the environment and the motivation of staff to teach skills and build relationships. As adults we do this best when we are calm and rational, and when we realise that our own behaviour and emotions can be a huge influence.

Whether or not a child has a 'behaviour difficulty' or a 'behavioural need' is not a fact. It is a belief of the adults associated with the child, based on their personal constructs and their understanding of socially defined criteria.

Young children will only be able to behave in a way that is
appropriate to their age and own stage of development.

3

Why Two-Year-Olds May Behave Differently to Three- and Four-Year-Olds

Early childhood is the time when children learn to think, learn about themselves in a social context and develop language – all at an astounding rate. The stage of development between the ages of two years and three years is a huge one. The whole early years period is a time in which children develop rapidly, socially, emotionally, intellectually and physically; during the year between ages two and three this development is even faster. Once a child is two the chances are that they will have begun to explore their environment, they are mobile, they are developing independence and they are starting to know what they want to do and conversely what they don't want to do. However, their social skills in terms of turn taking and sharing are not as strongly developed. They still have difficulty with waiting and ideally want things to happen for them immediately. Due to the fact that they are always 'on the go' they need a lot of sleep and can easily become cranky and fractious. Their language skills are not sufficiently developed for them to make their needs known and therefore they are more likely to have temper tantrums as a result of the combination of this and the other factors above. This phase isn't known as the 'terrible twos' without good reason. All this means they can be quite unpredictable. Two-year-olds tend to get frustrated easily and this can sometimes lead to destructive behaviours.

Young children will only be able to behave in a way that is appropriate to their own age and stage of development; so two-year-olds are unlikely to be able to behave in the same way as four-year-olds, not because they don't want to, but because they simply can't.

Concentration spans are different for two-year-olds compared to four-year-olds. Temper tantrums are more prevalent from about 18 months to two-and-a-half years than they are at four years old. However, each individual child is different so there are no hard and fast rules, only generalisations.

At the age of two children still have a tendency to play alongside others – engage in parallel play. They also find it difficult to see anything from another's perspective.

Two-year-olds benefit from the time and attention of adults within a setting – as do all children – however, once a child is older they are better able to express their needs and wishes and function more independently. Two-year-olds need time in order to develop these relationships and need more time to have their physical and emotional needs met and to create attachments. If adults know children well and take time to develop bonds, ensuring that they know they are valued, this helps children to develop their social and emotional capacity and consequently has an impact on their behaviour.

Extending young children's vocabulary is a key issue. At the age of two, children's language is developing at a fast pace. By enabling children to express their feelings and extend their language we enable them to better regulate their own behaviour.

Adults who understand young children's physical needs as well as their emotional needs – by getting to know the child well – can pre-empt difficulties; if you know a child is very tired you also know when little tantrums may be likely to occur. While this can be true of all small children it is more likely to occur with a two-year-old than a three- or four-year-old just because they tend to get tired more easily.

Two-year-olds are so much more egocentric than their older counterparts; supporting them in small group work to encourage turn-taking skills and language development is crucial. Giving them a secure and predictable environment scaffolded by an adult to develop skills, which in turn leads to the beginnings of the development of empathy, has an impact on their social and emotional skills, which in turn affects their behaviour within a setting. As the attention span of a two-year-old is much less than that of a three-year-old, any group activities need to be very short.

Additionally, two-year-olds tend to need more support at transition times. This is not just when they arrive and separate from the person who brings them to the setting, but within the session/s as they move from one activity to another, are requested to join an activity, and, for example, at tidy up time. If adults can give clear notice of these times and physically help them to move on by being a constant alongside them, this lessens the chances of the children failing to understand what is happening, and with it, the chances of them becoming upset or anxious.

Meal times with two-year-olds can also prove a challenge sometimes, as they are becoming increasingly independent and this is also a stage where food fads may well occur. This is something that can be anticipated; however, given two-year-olds' unpredictability it can be hard to manage. This is an area where working with parents is key.

Think and reflect

What is it like for a two-year-old in your setting?

Do they know they are a unique child?

How do they know and how do you know this is true?

Are their relationships positive ones?

4

Teaching Self-Regulation

This is about enabling children to recognise their emotions and organise their experiences in such a way that their needs are met. In the end, children need to be able to choose for themselves to behave in certain ways in certain situations. They need to be able to evaluate a situation using their senses and previous experiences and respond in the way that they feel is best. This doesn't need a separate curriculum; it isn't an isolated skill. It is something that can be developed through everyday experiences. It involves the ability to regulate both positive and negative emotions – the things we enjoy and make us happy as well as the things that upset us, make us angry or make us sad.

Among the skills and attributes needed to develop this are self-awareness, self-confidence, appropriate self-esteem, understanding and expressing your own feelings and developing an understanding of the feelings of others, an understanding that there are choices, the ability to make decisions and the ability to communicate effectively. Both academic learning and behavioural learning require well-developed skills of self-regulation.

Thought should be given as to when an adult withdraws support.

Teaching problem-solving skills is a big step towards independence. In everyday matters, such as putting on shoes or wellies or zipping up a coat, staff can scaffold the learning and help the child to get started.

Making choices about, for example, their snack supports children in learning to evaluate their likes and dislikes and teaches sharing and turn-taking skills, while helping to develop self-control. Pouring out their own drink from a jug and even serving drinks to others promotes independence, the ability to make choices, self-confidence and social skills.

The use of sand timers or a song at regular tidy up times, along with a set routine, teaches children to work together and to tidy away their belongings. This encourages respect for others and for the things in their environment.

Learning a new skill, such as threading, may help a child to begin to understand their own strengths and weaknesses. Taking turns in a game encourages the development of attention skills and the skill of waiting. Games need initially to be very short as attention spans are similarly short. Building towers with blocks so high that they eventually fall over and then starting again encourages persistence when faced with difficult problems; be careful though – at what point may frustration kick in?

When adults talk about their own emotions it can help children to access strategies to help them manage their own feelings, for example – 'I am feeling sad today because I can't go to my friend's birthday party tonight, but I am going to send her a nice card instead and I will see her next week.'

Giving a young child responsibilities, no matter how small, is likely to lead that child to behave in a more careful manner towards other people and belongings. The impact is not always immediate as it is a skill to be learned, but it is one well worth teaching!

Teaching small children self-regulation needs adults who are also aware of their own emotions and are able to self-regulate and reflect on children's individual needs. Adults are then able to model, prompt, hint and cue the child in so the child then learns for him or herself.

There are many more examples and none of this is terribly complicated; however, it does need conscious planning so that opportunities are not missed. Thought should be given as to when the adult withdraws their support. It's a bit like teaching a small child to ride a bicycle – at what point do you take your hand off the saddle?

5

What We Mean by Nurture

To me, nurture means looking after, caring for, helping to grow. We 'nurture' all sorts of things. We nurture plants – help them to grow strongly; we 'nurture' our own interests – develop them, hone them, become more proficient and knowledgeable. Those of us lucky enough to be parents 'nurture' our children to the best of our abilities, to help them to grow up into strong, healthy, caring human beings who can stand on their own two feet. This means meeting emotional needs as well as physical needs.

In schools and settings we try to offer a safe base where small children can grow and develop. Children need the unconditional love of a parent or caregiver and approval from those who are important to them. They respond best to clear signals so it is important that love and approval are made explicit. They also need security and for both their physical and emotional needs to be met. It is important to see each child as an individual and help to develop their skills from their own unique starting point. It is important to have a non-judgemental attitude

It is important to see children as individuals and develop skills from their own unique staring point.

and to maybe move away from 'normal' expectations of behaviour at any given age.

When adults listen – really listen – and then respond to small children, share activities, share food and so on, bonds are formed. When adults praise even the smallest of things, children respond and their self-esteem grows, along with the relationship with the caregiving adult. Through this the child's understanding of themselves and the world around them grows; they begin to develop empathy and sympathy and they blossom.

Children all see the world differently as a result of their life experiences to date. The quality of their early relationships is overwhelmingly important. Sometimes children have had difficult early relationships; by nurturing these children we can help build pathways to aid in their understanding of their world. Sometimes the experiences we give may need to be very similar to those we would give to a much younger child; emotional age is not always the same as chronological age. This is an important factor, but early childhood/baby experiences given in an age-appropriate way can sometimes help to shape the children we see at two, three, four, five years – and older.

Language is a way to express feelings. Sometimes, without the appropriate vocabulary to express themselves, children 'act out' their feelings. Using words instead of actions is another skill to be taught. Informally as well as formally the language of emotion is a great help in enabling communication and progressing social and emotional development. If you don't have a reasonable understanding of what 'happy' and 'sad' are, how do you know how to make another person happy?

Think of your own facial expressions; without words you can communicate a myriad of emotions. Small children need to learn to pick up on these visual cues. Having a mirror in your home corner or near the door of the setting and encouraging children to use it, make faces, show emotions and develop the associated language can be hugely successful. However, it takes time.

6

The Importance of Physical Environments and Their Impact on Behaviour

The quality of a child's learning environment is extremely important: both the indoor and the outdoor environment. Children need activity, sensory stimulation, fresh air and an appropriate diet, and young children in particular need a good balance of rest and activity. Given that all behaviour happens within a context it is possible to teach social, emotional and behavioural skills by modifying the environment. The actual quality of the environment is paramount – both the physical one and the emotional environment created by well-trained and sympathetic staff who strive to develop children's own skills.

An overwhelmingly noisy environment is likely to lead to a prevalence of shouting and noisy play. A silent one can stifle conversation and language development. Essentially it's about getting a balance – children being free to go and play outside, develop their enquiring, turn-taking and social skills, be loud and noisy, but then being able to come into a quieter environment and learn the sorts of behaviours acceptable there. This takes time –

Small children learn about themselves through their interactions with the environment.

and again the starting point depends on skills learned as a result of the child's previous experiences.

The nature and structure of the physical environment and the structure of the session/day impact on the child's view of their surroundings and the learning that is enabled through it. Predictable routines help to build security and self-confidence. Small children learn about themselves through their interactions with their environment.

We can scaffold learning by the areas and the equipment we offer. A comfortable couch in a book corner lends itself to sharing a book and sitting comfortably and quietly and aids the development of speaking and listening skills. We can enable children to be inquisitive and learn from their experiences; both indoor and outdoor areas are good for this but it depends what you put there!

The décor in a setting can have an impact. Think about the way you decorate your own home, and different rooms within it, to create the type of atmosphere you like and are comfortable with. Different rooms will often be decorated in different ways. Bright primary colours create a different atmosphere to pastels. 'Homely' doesn't necessarily mean shabby or overly chintzy. Bright lighting creates a different effect to subdued lighting.

Sharing and turn-taking skills can be developed if we consider the equipment we make available for any given activity: for example, a painting activity with shared paint pots in the centre of the table, a dough activity set up for four children with only three rolling pins and two cutters. With outside equipment, maybe agree a set number of turns on a bike and scooter and if possible provide equipment that two children can use together. Sometimes it is the simplest things that encourage children to develop the skills that they need. Planning for this is crucial though, as are staff skilled in observation, with a good knowledge of child development.

Young children tend to use the floor as much as they do furniture. What is your floor like? Two-year-olds generally find it hard to stay still, therefore access to both indoor and outdoor environments where they can constantly be on the move and explore and develop their skills at their own pace is essential. This is the same for all children. Hence – look at your indoor flooring. As well as being clean, is it fit for purpose? Is it interesting? Does it perhaps demark areas? Flooring can also have an impact on noise levels.

Developing pre-school children's independence is crucially important, teaching confidence, resilience and self-assurance in everyday tasks. Being able to do something for themselves is often a good motivator. Some children need more help in developing these skills than others.

Respect for equipment in any environment is a skill that may need to be taught. Children may well come across things that are new to them, perhaps a play workbench with hammers and drills, for example. You need to consider whether you want them to hammer and drill only on the workbench, or is it fine to hammer and drill bookcases, outdoor equipment and so on? There is a need to put some boundaries in place; while we want to develop creativity, we still need to develop respect.

The structure of the timetable in the setting is important – access to outdoor play early on in the session sometimes helps children settle to quieter activities afterwards.

Think and reflect

Does it make a difference if children play outside first thing?

If access to outdoor play space is at certain times only, what is the effect of moving those times? This is something you should test out.

Review your environment often. Is it stimulating?

Would it be interesting to you if you were a child?

Would you be motivated to learn here?

We all learn by watching and listening to others.

7

The Importance of Expectations and Teaching Positive Behaviour

As with anything, if we have high expectations of children's behaviour – given their age and understanding – we tend to get more positive outcomes. If we praise and reinforce the behaviours we would ideally like to see, try our best to ignore some of the ones we would really rather didn't happen and concentrate on teaching skills, it generally makes for a happier environment. We need to have realistic beliefs; we can only seek to influence children's behaviour – we can't actually change it ourselves. The reward for positive behaviour should be the fact that the children have a happier time. Adults should be constantly vigilant and notice all the children who are behaving in appropriate ways, catching them 'being good' and commenting with specific praise both verbally and non-verbally. Verbal praise can be used to develop a child's intrinsic motivation: 'Well done, you have completed that jigsaw. I am sure you could do a harder one.' Sometimes, however, we may need to additionally reward certain children when they have learned the skills to behave in a way that comes more naturally to other children whose skill set is already more highly developed. In fact, tangible rewards for all children as a concrete way of telling them how pleased we are with them are a good thing – although they do need to be linked to emotional feedback. As adults we appreciate when somebody says thank you to us or maybe gives us a little something for our efforts. Small children are no different. Rewards shouldn't be seen as bribes. They are simply a way of acknowledging something that has been done well or a new skill that has been learned. They are a way of building up confidence and developing appropriate self-esteem.

Positive behaviour needs to be taught. Adults need to model it, both to children and among themselves. Adults can't really expect nursery children to put coats on before going outside if they do not also put their own on. When adults in a nursery or reception class setting speak to each other, if they don't say please and thank you, children cannot be expected to do the same. When adults model helping behaviours, children watch, listen and have a chance to copy.

When modelling behaviours it is sometimes useful for the adults to do this in a slightly exaggerated manner. Adults are showing children what to do. Sometimes children don't notice. Young children are egocentric and absorbed in themselves and learn gradually about the world around them and how to interact with it. As adults in a setting, if we praise each other and do it in a noticeable but still genuine way, children do realise. If we do the same thing in a hushed whisper, nobody other than the adult we are speaking to is aware so there is no opportunity provided for copying.

Model the behaviour that you wish to see. Try not to overemphasise the behaviours that you don't. This may seem very obvious but actually adults' behaviour is a highly significant influence within a setting. Act as a role model for small children who are in the process of developing their own social skills and their ability to make choices. You don't have to be perfect – we all make mistakes, but if you do make one, apologise.

Young children very quickly pick up on adults' behaviour; they watch, listen, absorb and do pick up on what is expected. Tone of voice is important as they tune into this. They also very quickly pick up on who responds to them, and in which ways, dependent on what they are doing. Consider the language between adults in your setting. Listen for a session and see what the adults are actually saying and how.

Think and reflect

Is there anything you need to change?

Where staff consistently model the same positive approaches children pick up on this more quickly, the general behaviour within the setting becomes more positive and everybody is happier. Consistency really is key – not because it is focussed on during inspections, but because children (and adults) need to feel secure and know where they stand. Inconsistent expectations confuse children – and staff as well! Obviously at times we need to differentiate expectations and approaches because of individual needs; but, overall, practice needs to be positive and very consistent, so there is no room for confusion.

Where staff model positive behaviours to other staff the approach becomes even more consistent. We all learn by watching and listening to others. If you have an approach that you find works, tell your colleagues; let them test it out for themselves.

Be aware of your own body language: the way that you sit, stand, walk; the way you enter the setting at the start of your working day. If you move purposefully you present as being more confident. Body language communicates a high proportion of any message; subtleties like raising your eyebrows, hand gestures and facial expressions all contribute. Folding your arms can be said to create a barrier; a more open posture invites people in. Young children are learning to read body language as they learn to respond to spoken language. Think about yours.

When adults do have to intervene because they see something that is inappropriate within the context it is useful to do it in a 'least to most intrusive' way. This means – unless of course the situation is dangerous – staff make the smallest intervention first.

Focussing attention on the children behaving appropriately – catching children 'being good' while ignoring the one who hasn't quite got round to it yet – can be a useful starting point: 'Oh, well done, Fred and George. I can see that you have started to tidy up the small world, thank you' (while keeping an eye on Emma who is busy getting it all out again). If Emma then realises that it is tidy up time and starts to do the same thing, make sure you say thank you to her as well.

Using your own physical proximity is another useful least intrusive strategy. You don't have to say anything. Sometimes moving towards the child who is doing the thing you would rather they did not do will work in prompting them to behave in a more positive way. If you go just about close enough to nearly invade their personal space so they definitely notice you are there, but not so close that your actions can cause anxiety, often the child's behaviour will change. Again, make a positive comment when it does.

Using simple questions to refocus, gently approach the child and ask them a question not related to the behaviour you would rather not see: 'That looks good, Laura, are you using the blue paint or the red paint?' (she is busy tipping the blue paint out all over the floor). 'Yes, that's right blue – go and find me some blue bricks out of that box while I just tidy up this paint so people don't slip in it.'

Give a clear rule reminder: 'Keith, remember our walking rule.' He stops running. 'Good boy, that's excellent walking.' Remember to say exactly what behaviour is 'good'; make your praise specific. 'Good boy' by itself is not as effective.

The tone of your voice is important here – if you adapt your voice levels and tone appropriately to match your message there is a greater chance of the message getting through. Mood can be altered relatively easily by altering the tone of your voice.

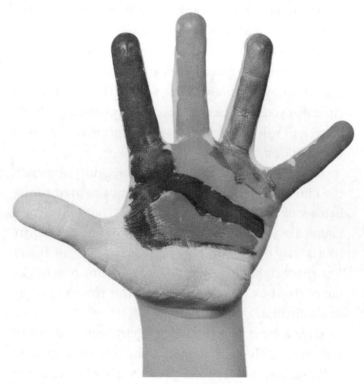

Young children are likely to need help in resolving conflict.

8

Focussing on Primary Behaviours

A primary behaviour is the first behaviour you would rather not see in a situation where you have to intervene. An example might be Fred snatching a toy or piece of equipment from Paolo. This is completely unprovoked; he just goes up to Paolo who is playing happily and whizzes it out of his hands. Paolo bursts into tears and tries to get it back. Fred runs off, throws the piece of equipment on the floor, stamps on it and breaks it. Your primary behaviour in this case is the snatching: the first incident. It is easy to get drawn in and focus on the issue of breaking it. It is the same if a child ends up talking back to you. The talking back is not the primary behaviour – don't get drawn in!

Focus on the primary behaviour – the snatching – because if the snatching hadn't happened in the first place it wouldn't have led to the toy being broken.

Young children are just beginning to learn about the consequences of their own actions for themselves and for others, but we can't assume these concepts are secure. They may well not be able to put themselves in the other child's place. They are likely to require help in resolving conflict. Adults can help by trying to get each child to describe or show what happened and by making sure that they very obviously listen to both sides of the story when accounts differ. It is useful to reflect back what the child has said: 'So, Paolo, you are sad because you were playing with the toy and Fred took it.' 'You got angry/sad, Fred because you wanted to play with that toy.' Sometimes very young children only have developing concepts of the meaning of the words happy and sad – it depends on the child – but be aware of this. Angry and sad may be the same thing to Fred at this stage. Depending on the children's understanding, it can be helpful to ask their opinion as to what should happen next – along with a rule reminder: 'Remember, Fred, we play nicely with our friends in nursery.'

9

Rights, Rules and Relationships

Within any setting everyone has rights – children and adults. Take these four basic rights, which should underpin your behaviour policy:

1. Children's right to learn.
2. Your right to teach/develop/instruct.
3. Everybody's right to safety.
4. Everybody's right to dignity and respect.

These allow you and your children to feel safe. This framework enables you to make decisions about your response to children's behaviour. It enables you to go beyond, 'Do it because I told you to.'

Settings have rules; a few simple ones are best, ones that work equally as well in the outdoor environment as in the indoor one. Rules should sit within the behaviour policy of the establishment, which should conform to any current government guidance. Rules should be phrased positively, for example, 'We speak nicely to each other' as opposed to 'Do not shout', 'We walk inside' as opposed to 'Do not run'. Rules should describe the behaviour we wish to see. Rules should be displayed pictorially and in

Build relationships over time through simple actions.

simple text in all areas of the setting or nursery class. As with other displays they should be positioned at child height. They should be relatively large and prominent. Something A4 size stuck on the side of a bookcase is not appropriate.

Rules need to be actively taught, spoken about, acted out, painted, used in role play and so on. Your rules will require a level of understanding in order to be followed, and children tend not to pick them up by osmosis; they need to be taught the necessary skills in a very practical and concrete way. Rules – and also routines, for example putting boots on before going outside, taking boots off when coming inside, hanging coats and painting aprons up – all need to be taught and revisited over and over again. This is not something for the beginning of term – it is something that is ongoing. Predictable regular routines – with sometimes slightly elastic boundaries – and warnings of transitions are important in making sure children feel secure. Reviewing your routines is a useful thing to do. Think about why you have them and the skills that they teach.

Think and reflect

Are your routines fit for purpose?

Rules need to be reinforced constantly and in the most concrete and practical way. For example, if a new toy or puppet is introduced to the setting it can help if the children explain the rules to it to make sure it gets on well with everybody. Large glove puppets are excellent for this and they can be made to behave inappropriately; children will delight in telling the puppet what it should do instead. Puppets are also extremely useful for explaining routines and appropriate behaviour outside and can be used to act out short scenarios. I used to have a large orange crow puppet called Stone. As well as periodically trying to peck children, Stone also became sad from time to time and the children suggested ways to help him and make him feel better.

The purpose of the rules is so that staff can refer to them when they see children keeping them. Rules are definitely not there in order for staff (and other children) to catch children when they break them. Catch them being 'good'. Catch them keeping the rules and give immediate positive feedback if possible; if this is not possible, make sure that you tell the child at a later stage in the session that you saw them doing whatever they did and that you are so pleased with them. This works so much better than telling children off when they inadvertently – or sometimes deliberately – fail to follow the setting rules. If you notice and praise the behaviours that you want to see you will get more of them. Confrontational styles can produce adverse reactions. Having rules to refer to scaffolds staff responses. Actively looking for children keeping the rules makes such a difference to the tone of a setting. Test it out – catch them following one of your rules and comment positively and specifically when you notice. Have a look at the impact on the child concerned, the children near them, and on yourself and other staff. What do you notice?

Although it may seem overly simplistic, just by concentrating on using positive language, and by using it frequently, adults can have an impact on children's behaviour. Describe the behaviours you want to see.

We all tend to function more happily within the context of positive relationships. Babies form relationships with their primary caregiver from the moment they are born and develop a bond. Small children form relationships with their family and friends and extend these relationships when they meet new children and adults in their early years setting.

Relationships that value others will raise self-esteem and help them to grow. Relationships in settings between children and children, children and adults and between adults and adults are all important to consider. Perhaps the adult-to-adult relationships between those who work with young children are the most important because they help set the tone of the setting and the tone of the other two types of relationship. When relationships between adults are supportive and positive a whole lot more is achieved. We build relationships over time with children and adults when we do fairly simple things – when we greet people by name, when we stop and have a little chat, when we make eye contact and give them our full attention, even if it is only for a minute, and when we remind both children and adults of something they have done well. We should treat children with the same degree of respect as we believe we ourselves are due. Even when we need to correct them or remind them of a setting rule we should maintain their dignity and protect their self-esteem. Sometimes we have to consciously build relationships with children, and when we build relationships with parents and carers the same is true.

10

Observing Behaviour Within a Setting

It is as important to observe positive behaviour as it is to observe the behaviours that you would rather did not occur. When we mention 'observing behaviour' the first thing that tends to spring to mind is that we are going to observe and look for the problems. It is as important to look for a child's strengths and interests, in order to be able to build on them, as it is to look for the things they may be doing 'wrong'. Observation by adults builds empathy and aids planning. Stepping back and observing the things that are going well is time very well spent and none of us do this often enough.

The very word 'behaviour' is subjective. Therefore, it is important to get a view that is as unbiased as possible. Unwanted behaviour in children generally causes emotional reactions in adults. However, adults' reactions are different depending on their own world view. For instance, some adults find swearing very offensive, particularly when small children are involved; for other adults it may be spitting that pushes their buttons. It is important to be aware of what pushes your own buttons – the things you

What pushes your buttons?

dislike most – because you may be more liable to react to these sorts of behaviours than others.

Any persistent unwanted behaviours are wearing. Staff get worn down; they almost anticipate the next incident. This again impacts on staff behaviour – sometimes it can become a self-fulfilling prophecy.

The use of a basic checklist is a help here. Look at things the child can do – can they repeat instructions; follow a one- or two-part verbal instruction; collect equipment for a task; stay on task for two, five, ten minutes; value completed work, construction and so on; follow routines; gain the attention of adults appropriately; take turns; sit appropriately for a short story; respond to praise; take responsibility for a job; tidy up when asked; keep their hands and feet to themselves; make positive comments to peers; initiate and maintain friendships; use appropriate table manners? Focus on what they are able to do in the broadest sense rather than anything that might be causing them a bit of a problem. This gives you a baseline at a particular point in time within a particular context. Don't forget to date the form!

This should be followed by an actual observation. Your basic checklist should have given you an indication as to which sorts of behaviours/skills may be of concern and would potentially need support to develop, and this might help you with further observations. Only note the behaviours you actually see in clear, observable terms; for example, not 'Chris was being naughty', but 'Chris bit John at snack time'. Make sure you include them all, exactly as you see them; don't discount any because you can 'explain' why the child behaves in this way. Maybe observe for three quarters of an hour, tally positive and negative behaviours and look at interactions, adult and child initiated. Look at facial expressions and body language too. Make a note of context, time of day, temperature and noise level. As well as observing the child themselves you are observing the setting as a whole, though in a more general way. As well as noting frequency of behaviours, look for persistency and severity. Then ideally come back and look at the same child again another time. Compare your findings.

You are looking to create an impartial baseline – something that is as objective as possible – in order to see which skills you need to develop next. If you don't feel you can necessarily be impartial (there is nothing wrong with this), consider asking somebody else within the context to observe for you, or do a paired observation.

Don't forget to observe the reactions the child receives from both staff and other children. Remember that all behaviour has a reason and one person's behaviour impacts on another's.

Think and reflect

Sometimes children are looking for a reaction – does this give you any insight into the reasons why the child behaved as they did?

When you have identified a basic skill that you think would make a difference then set out how you are going to teach it. You might have identified several skills, but choose one or maybe two priorities. Concerns which potentially endanger the safety of the child, other children and staff will need to come high on the list.

Think and reflect

What situations are you going to create for the child to learn and practise this skill?

You will have to do it many times – how are you going to know when the new skill has been learned?

How exactly are you going to teach it?

Look at this same skill about six weeks after you have actively tried to teach it in the way in which you decided.

Observing social relationships in general within a setting is a helpful thing to do.

Discussing your ideas with colleagues is essential, as you all need to understand which skills you are trying to develop in order to have a consistent approach.

However, when talking about this, don't forget to mind your language when you describe behaviour! 'Cheeky' means different things to different people – describe the behaviour you see. 'Keith told Mrs Graham she had dropped her dinner down her front while she was eating her lunch' – this tells you exactly what Keith did. It is so much better than, 'Keith was rude to Mrs Graham.' If your colleague tells you, 'Sue has been very aggressive this morning' you need to find out exactly what she did here because 'aggressive' is a very woolly term!

Think and reflect

How do the toddlers in your setting reach out to each other and make contact?

How is their behaviour at two years old different from the behaviour of others at four years old?

How do they approach each other?

How do they attempt to make friends?

Are some children in the setting more 'popular' than others?

Who leads and who follows – and why do you think this may be?

11

Antecedents, Behaviour and Consequences

Sometimes, for a one-off incident, staff find that looking at the situation in terms of antecedents, behaviour and consequences is helpful. The antecedents are what was happening immediately before – for example, before one child kicked another on the floor.

Think and reflect

What was going on?

What were the antecedents in terms of the aggressor – what were they doing?

Did you hear anything said?

Who was there?

What was the noise level, temperature and so on like?

What time of day was it?

There may be no need to use overly complicated methods to help
improve a child's social, emotional and behavioural skills.

Make it broader than the 'incident' itself. By focussing your attention on what happened before – the antecedents – and what the outcome was, the consequences can often be far more effective than focussing energy on the 'event' itself.

Think and reflect

Are there any noticeable antecedents for the victim?

Has this child ever been a victim before?

What were the antecedents for staff – who was nearest?

What were they doing?

Then for the behaviour itself – given the behaviour that you actually saw – what happened?

Again for all three – the aggressor, victim and staff – what did they do? And what were the immediate consequences for all three?

Sometimes this is helpful in trying to make sense of a situation. It may be worth repeating if the same child is concerned in further incidents as sometimes a pattern begins to emerge. Sometimes it doesn't, but at least in considering the situation in this way you stand to gain some small insights and can plan better for the future.

Often there may be no need to use overly complicated methods to improve a child's behavioural skills. When you have identified an area for development it may mean that by changing the antecedents you can impact on the undesired behaviour. For example, you can pre-empt the situation, make sure you have communicated clear expectations or give an early warning. You can change the background/context in which the behaviour occurs, remove temptation, change the setting or, for some children, perhaps introduce an agreed prompt.

If there is a consequence to a child's behaviour it is important that the child understands that it is the behaviour that you don't like and that can't happen here, but you still like them as a person. Separate the behaviour from the person. It is important to keep relationships intact and focus on how to move on. Always protect the child's self-esteem.

It is also important to give children take-up time when you give them an instruction. Small children can get so engrossed in what they are doing that they do not even notice what is going on around them. Using their name before an instruction can be helpful – with a little pause to let it sink in that you are talking to them: 'Emma (pause), Emma, it is tidy up time now.' If you say thank you after an instruction it gives the impression that you expect compliance: 'Charlie (pause), Charlie, put the train in the box, thanks.' 'Chris (pause), put the plant in the hole now, thanks.'

Don't get caught with your plans down!

12

The Importance of Having a Plan When It All Goes Wrong

Imagine your worst-case scenario – what is the very worst thing that could happen to you in your setting concerning a child not behaving as you would ideally like? Is it somebody turning tables over, running amok and swearing at you? Is it something else? Imagine something awful and almost outside the realms of possibility! Even though you may be sure this would never happen it is extremely important to consider that it could. Make a plan. Talk through the plan with a colleague. Now you will never be caught without a plan! This ensures that adults don't react emotionally in the worst-case scenario situation. This is crucial. Their emotions do not come into play, they just follow the plan. Unwanted behaviours are often emotive and can push buttons. By planning for them we take away the element of surprise, take the shock and emotion on the adult's behalf out of the situation and whatever follows is far calmer, reasoned and logical.

All too often we may not see our own strengths.

13

Staff Feelings

It is hard to show generous and caring behaviours if you don't feel cared for and valued yourself and also if you don't actually value yourself both inside and outside work.

Everyone feels better when they receive positive feedback. If staff are modelling positive relationships and behaviour within the setting it is important to feed back to them the aspects of this that they do well. They then tend to do it more. It is also useful to consider how the setting as a whole achieves consistency in terms of supporting social and emotional development. Staff are role models for children so they should be well motivated and eager to learn, as they will then inspire the children they work with to be self-motivated about their own learning.

If staff have particular strengths it can be useful to play to them while developing areas in which they feel less confident. Some staff are perfectly happy asking for support, others less so. In the same way as we recognise children's strengths and acknowledge them we should encourage staff to recognise their own strengths and build on them. If you ask an adult what they do well in a work situation, they often find it difficult to answer you. If you observe, then tell them about the things they are good at they may initially find it embarrassing but as with children, a positive approach works much better than a negative one. All too often we do not see our own strengths. If there are areas that staff struggle with, taking a solution-focussed approach to the situation (or aspects of this approach) can often effectively move it on. For example, if a member of staff has had a difficult time supporting a small child to behave appropriately, scaling techniques can help: 'On a scale of nought to ten, where ten is the best it could be and nought is the opposite, how well do you think you managed the situation with Laura this morning?' 'That's great, three, is there anything you would do differently next time to make it a four?' The number given in the scaling is itself unimportant; the main thing is that the member of staff identifies an action to increase their score by a point, or even a half point!

When difficult situations do occur, all staff should calm themselves before they calm others. The best outcomes are rarely achieved when people are worked up.

14

Building Trust with Children and Parents

Babies and small children begin to develop a sense of behaviour in the home – this is where they develop their first insights into the feelings of others.

It is often said that parents and carers know their own children best. They have the closest relationships with the child. There is no training to be a parent, and parenting every child is different as every child has a different personality. You have to learn on the job and what suits one child does not always suit another. This is true of siblings as well as children from different families! No matter how much experience of children a person has had before becoming a parent themselves, looking after your own child can be challenging and frustrating as well as wonderful and rewarding. There is a need for flexibility and an understanding and an acknowledgement that there is no such thing as a perfect parent. We can only be 'good enough'.

Relationships with parents need to be positive and honest. At times this may mean not denying that their child has skills to learn. Some parents may need support in helping to develop their child's social and emotional

Children don't come with instruction manuals.

skills and early years settings may be the first place where this topic of conversation has been broached, therefore it needs to be done with great sensitivity.

Social disadvantage, homelessness, low socio-economic status, poverty, overcrowding, social isolation, maternal depression and exposure to violence can lead to difficulties parenting and consequently in some cases to conduct difficulties in children. It is important to realise that this is not always the case, and where elements of the above come into play early years settings can be extremely helpful in building relationships with parents and supporting them in small ways, while protecting the parent's self-esteem as they would their child's. It is important to remember that when a parent or carer arrives at the setting to pick up or drop off their child you do not know what they may have gone through to get there. You may never know.

It can on some occasions be useful to sensitively suggest strategies for the parent to test out at home, while emphasising that all of these need persistence and none of them is a magic wand! If a parent has a child who they find difficult in a particular shop, for example, suggesting the parent avoids the situation for a little while instead of persisting with actions that are causing them anxiety can be useful. It is quite justifiable to avoid things – sometimes we need to be given permission. Sometimes demonstrating to parents how to encourage their child to do the right thing can be very useful, telling them what they should say, for example: 'Don't pull the dog's ears, stroke him on his back like this…' The same sorts of warning and distraction strategies you use in the setting also work at home: 'It's time for your bath in five minutes after this programme has finished.' 'Right, come on, who wants a drink? Come with me and get it.' The most effective is catching the child 'being good', doing the right thing and giving attention and affirmation for that: 'It's lovely seeing you playing so nicely' is much better than 'Stop it', 'Be quiet', 'Stop fighting'. However, it can be hard: sometimes if an adult is alone with a small child for a substantial part of the day it is difficult for them to see the things that the child is doing well.

Parents often want to give their children rewards for 'doing the right thing'. It is important to stress that these rewards need only be small, and that maybe the parent's time is the best reward of all. There is often no need for expensive material rewards. A cuddle on the sofa, a walk to a park, an extra-long story time – often people don't think of these simple things, which children really love and are so crucial for the development of positive well-being.

15

Ten Very Important Things to Remember

1. None of us are perfect.

2. Behaviour can be taught; it's a skill.

3. Children develop at different rates.

4. Chronological age is not necessarily the same as emotional age.

5. Young children thrive on nurturing relationships.

6. Adults' perception of 'appropriate' behaviour is different.

7. Behaviour is situational – the context can be altered.

8. It is necessary to have clear plans based on firm foundations in order to develop social, emotional and behavioural skills.

9. Children's behaviour is often not personal to the adults who live or work with them.

10. Tomorrow is another day.

Promoting positive behaviour within early years settings can be challenging at times. Staff support little individuals and their parents, all of whom are different, so there are no definitive answers.

This book sets out some brief strategies and areas to consider in the hope that it is practically useful.

The ability to see behaviour as a set of skills which need to be taught within a context is a great help, as is the ability to focus on the positive and to see tomorrow as another day.

Index